STEAM

Steam

PORTRAITS OF THE GREAT DAYS OF THE BRITISH STEAM LOCOMOTIVE

Edited by Geoffrey Kichenside

DAVID & CHARLES

NEWTON ABBOT · LONDON · NORTH POMFRET (VT) · VANCOUVER

ISBN 0 7153 7070 7
Library of Congress Catalog Card Number 75-10532

Set in Univers
and printed in Great Britain
by Alden & Mowbray Limited, Oxford
for David & Charles (Holdings) Limited
South Devon House, Newton Abbot, Devon

Published in the United States of America
by David & Charles Inc
North Pomfret Vermont 05053 USA

Published in Canada
by Douglas David & Charles Limited
132 Philip Avenue North Vancouver BC

Introduction

The steam locomotive served Britain for almost a century and a half. While in a few countries, mostly in Southern Africa, the Indian sub-continent and the Far East, it survives in ordinary everyday service, in Britain its role in normal all-year-round commercial use ended in August 1968. Yet it survives in Britain on the many privately-operated branch railways and working steam museums and depots up and down the country by the untiring dedication of small groups of hard-working enthusiasts who have set out to keep steam locomotives alive, and which delight hundreds of thousands of visitors each year. From time to time express steam locomotives which escaped the cutters torch and now mostly in private hands can be seen in much of their former glory at the head of special excursions on selected British Railways main lines.

After early attempts by the Cornish pioneer Trevithick in the construction of a self-propelled steam machine soon after the turn of the nineteenth century, other engineers developed the theme with primitive engines on colliery railways in North and North East England. Out of their basic work grew the steam locomotives which were sufficiently promising to be used on the Stockton & Darlington Railway from its opening in 1825, an event generally reckoned to be the start of what became the British Railways network of today, and certainly the first public railway in the world to use steam locomotives.

Nevertheless, locomotives of the 1820s and 1830s were hardly reliable machines and some of the collieries which tried them reverted to horses, but it was clear that the steam engine could be made into a machine which could outrun and outdistance the horse, and haul much greater loads.

By 1840 when the new trunk lines from London were in operation steam locomotives were reaching speeds of 40, even 50mph on some lines, with loads of 50 tons and over and running on journeys of 100 miles and more. During the next 30 years steam locomotives gradually developed in shape and size to types familiar in our own times, although it was well into the present century before really large express locomotives were built to take full advantage of the maximum sizes and weights permitted by platform and tunnel clearances and the track. The turning point really came with the new century, for during the previous decade so many of the features which today we take for granted in passenger comfort — heating, electric lighting, restaurant cars, corridors and toilet facilities — were only then being introduced, on one or two trains at first and then on a general scale. This meant heavier trains which in turn brought the need for larger, more powerful locomotives. Until then many express trains were lightweight affairs, and locomotive builders were able to exercise their talents in graceful design rather than super power.

The 1920s and 1930s were the years when the publicity men got to work on the railways. This was the era of the crack express, named of course and the pride of the line, when trains were clean and always ran to time or so it seemed. Then came the second world war and the run down of equipment with lack of maintenance, and harsh treatment for which locomotives were not designed. Yet the railways recovered and for a short while there was a resurgence of steam after nationalisation with new designs in the 1950s. They lasted little more than a decade until at last, area by area, the steam locomotive gave way to diesels and electrics, and the last regular steam-hauled trains ran in North West England in August 1968.

The steam locomotive was undoubtedly one of man's finest achievements. It was so much like a living thing: it had a will of its own, it could be stubborn, it could be sweet tempered, it could ride as roughly as a bucking bronco or it could be as smooth as a Rolls Royce. Looked after and well fed with good coal it was a superb piece of machinery; neglected and run down it was called all the names under the sun. Yet it usually got you home even if it was ailing. A hefty clout with a coal hammer often helped in the miraculous recovery of an erratic component. Try that with a modern diesel!

The sound and sight of a steam locomotive in action is something that once experienced is never forgotten. Visually and audibly it is almost an art form. In this album steam locomotives are portrayed in action from the last century to the end of regular steam operation and in preserved form to the present time. With so many locomotives and such a long period to cover it can be no more than a glimpse, a selection of old and not so old from many parts of the country, which will bring back memories and help to mark a century and a half of steam.

Frontispiece

A typical end of platform scene repeated thousands of times every day in the age of steam with the fireman looking back to see that all is well as the locomotive comes to life and gets the train on the move. In this case the engine is Hall class 4-6-0 No 6974 *Bryngwyn Hall* seen here leaving Bath with a summer saturday extra to Weston-super-Mare on 9 September 1961.   *G. A. Richardson*

Summer saturday extras during the 1950s often
meant that engines which ought to have been
pensioned off years before were pressed into service
even though they were not in tip-top condition. This
is Euston on the sunny afternoon of 13 July 1957
with compound 4-4-0 No 41162 struggling with the
heavy 3.05pm Euston to Northampton. Although
they were built in the early 1920s and put up some
good performances on Euston-Birmingham trains
during the next decade, by the late 1950s their
appearances on the Euston line were rare.

G. M. Kichenside

The mainstay of the principal express services from
Euston for much of the decade or so before the
second world war were the Royal Scot 4-6-0s which
when built in 1927 were the largest and most
powerful locomotives ever to have performed
regularly on the line. They were capable of some
feats of heavy haulage and often tackled 15 coach
trains or more on Liverpool, Manchester, or Glasgow
services. Here No 6112 *Sherwood Forester* storms
slowly up the climb from the platform end at Euston
for the first mile to Camden in 1935.

British Railways

The former London & North Western main line from Euston to the North West was well endowed with water troughs to allow locomotives to take water at speed. The first set was at Bushey, less than 16 miles after the start from Euston. One of the British Railways standard class 7 Britannia Pacifics, No 70021 *Morning Star*, heads an up freight over the troughs in the early 1960s.

Gerald T. Robinson

In contrast, the same location 70 years earlier. This is a remarkable photograph for it was taken out of the back of one train, running neck and neck with a second train on a parallel line. The overflowing tender adds to the dramatic effect of sound and fury. The engine is one of Webb's compound 2-2-2-0s of the Jeanie Deans class. The bridge in this photograph is the one that was used by the photographer of the print on the facing page. The two tracks on the far left of the facing picture were later additions in 1912/13.

R. W. Hamilton Collection

A typical turn-of-the-century train on the Euston main line, this one an express for Liverpool double headed, as indeed most LNWR expresses were at that time, by a 2-2-2 with 8ft single driving wheels piloting a Jeanie Deans 2-2-2-0. The LNWR had some delightful names for most of its express locomotives although the leading one here of the Lady of the Lake class No 117 is more mundanely called *Tiger*.

Locomotive & General Railway Photographs

One of the reasons why Dr Beeching said that much of the British Railways system did not pay. Seemingly miles from nowhere Ivatt class 4 2-6-0 No 43049, one of the last designs built by the LMS before it was swallowed up into the nationalised British Railways network, passes the time of day playing with a few wagons at Kirkby Stephen East on 31 July 1967.

John Goss

The Midland Railway did not believe in large engines and if you had a heavy train you simply put on a second locomotive. A feature of the coal trains worked south from the Nottinghamshire coal fields was the fact that for many years they were nearly always worked by two engines as here in 1936 with a pair of 0-6-0s leaving a smokescreen across all tracks near Elstree.

C. R. L. Coles

A study in light and shade as BR standard Britannia
class 7 4-6-2 No 70017 *Arrow* makes steady progress
through the Lune Gorge in typical Lake District
showery weather with a Manchester-Glasgow train
in the early 1960s.   *J. S. Whiteley*

On the Midland route through the Pennines from
Carlisle to Leeds in the last full year of steam
working in the North West Britannia 4-6-2 No 70010
Owen Glendower climbs steadily up the final section
towards Ais Gill summit high in the northern
Pennine moorlands on 5 February 1967 with a
football special.   *John Goss*

The main line between Euston and Glasgow did not
include the steepest climbs on a British main line but
it had some long tough gradients which caused no
end of problems to freight trains, in particular, in
reaching the 900-1000ft or so summits. One was
over the Lakeland Fells at Shap and the other in the
Southern Uplands at Beattock across the border in
Scotland . Most freight trains and a few passenger
trains as well needed a second engine attached to
give them a helping hand and even then the steepest
parts of the climb at 1 in 75 pulled speed down on
occasions to little more than a crawl. It was
particularly bad in wet weather when driving wheels
fought a battle for adhesion and spun wildly, a
problem which even today occasionally affects the
electrically-hauled trains on this route. Our scene is
set a decade ago on 1 June 1966, first as a freight
train approaches hauled by class 5 4-6-0 No 45481,
and as it disappears in the distance past Scout Green
signalbox banked in the rear by 2-6-4T No 42110
leaving a smoke trail across the Fells.

M. C. Kemp

The Midland Railway route from Leeds to Carlisle
known as the Settle & Carlisle is one of the bleakest
in Britain as it passes across the Pennine chain over
Ais Gill summit, for much of the route lies across
bleak treeless wind-swept open moorland. Parts
are among the most isolated anywhere in Britain.
Its civil engineering structures were a challenge to
nature and stand out all the more against the
moorland setting. Here are two shots of LMS general
purpose class 5 4-6-0s as they head north across
Ribblehead viaduct on 14 October 1966. *John Goss*

Railways in Scotland were built through equally
inhospitable country in places, particularly the lines
through the Highlands, and also in the Uplands in
South West Scotland. This area forms the backdrop
for a Stranraer-Glasgow relief approaching Pinmore
behind BR standard class 4 2-6-0 No 76001 and a
class 5 4-6-0 on 31 July 1965.   *John Goss*

The Settle & Carlisle line abounds in bridges and
viaducts to span the numerous streams coming down
from the moors. One of BR's heavy freight 2-10-0s
No 92249 heads a block load of anhydrite from
Long Meg sidings near Lazonby, to Widnes on 1 June
1966.   *M. C. Kemp*

One of the less successful of BR standard designs was
the Clan class of which only 10 were built. The last
of the class No 72009 *Clan Stewart* leaves a smoke
trail over the moors near Beattock summit with the
9.25 Crewe-Perth/Aberdeen on 11 August 1964.

John S. Whiteley

The power and fury of class 5 4-6-0 No 45176 is
clearly visible as it struggles to get a coal train
assisted by a banking engine in the rear, towards
Beattock summit on 28 March 1964.

John S. Whiteley

Top Left
One of the most graceful locomotive designs ever was Patrick Stirling's 4-2-2 built in the 1870s for the principal Great Northern expresses from Kings Cross. With their 8ft diameter single driving wheels and outside cylinders they did not seem to need much effort in keeping their trains moving at quite a fair speed. Here No 53 heads an express including a dining car through the snowy North London suburbs in the 1890s.

Locomotive & General Railway Photographs

Bottom Left
Further north on the East Coast main line the North Eastern Railway handled much of its traffic with 4-4-0s by the turn of the century. They were handsome machines in mid-green livery with black and white lining and polished fittings as indeed were many locomotives at this time. A pair led by class M1 No 1629 are seen leaving York for the north in 1900 with a heavily laden East Coast route express formed largely of non-corridor six-wheel coaches but including a pair of restaurant cars in the middle.

Locomotive & General Railway Photographs

Above
Contrasting starkly with the locomotives depicted on the facing page is one of Gresley's streamlined class A4 4-6-2s, one of which, *Mallard*, happily preserved, holds the world's speed record for steam traction of 126mph achieved in 1938. Several other locomotives of this class have been preserved in working order both in Britain and abroad including No 60007 *Sir Nigel Gresley* seen here emerging from Gasworks Tunnel in a cloud of steam from the cylinder drain cocks soon after leaving Kings Cross with The White Rose express for Leeds on 26 April 1963.

Gerald T. Robinson

Freight is the life blood of the railway and nowhere more so than in the North East, the birthplace of railways as we know them today more than a century and a half ago. Coal features prominently and so too does iron ore, imported into this part of Britain at Tyne Dock and conveyed in block loads of specially constructed wagons to Consett Steel Works which is only a short run, but the gradients are severe and trains needed banking assistance. Heavy freight 2-10-0 No 92060 heads a loaded ore train towards Consett on 13 August 1965, banked behind by a diesel locomotive. *John Goss*

Fog is one of the railwayman's greatest hazards and was made worse in steam days when steam and smoke from the locomotive mingled to reduce visibility even further. It was just such a day on 1 October 1956 at Seaton in Co Durham as class J27 0-6-0 No 65885 creeps slowly forward with empty wagons for Hawthorns Colliery. *John Goss*

For several hundred years railways of sorts have been used to carry coal from collieries to waterways. Former North Eastern Railways class Q6 0-8-0 No 63346 continues the tradition as, with safety valves lifting, it drifts slowly down from Hawthorns Colliery to Sunderland on 15 October 1966. A sister engine in this class has been preserved and can be seen running on the North Yorkshire Moors Railway at Grosmont. *John Goss*

The steam locomotive with its many and varied tricks of smoke and steam exhaust, depending on weather conditions, provided photographers with plenty of scope for out of the ordinary shots, particularly against the light photographs such as this one of a coal train winding slowly through the western approaches of Newcastle Central in mid 1960s. *Malcolm Dunnett*

All appears to have been safely gathered in as LNER class B1 4-6-0 No 61263, a design which appeared during the second world war for mixed traffic duties leaves St Andrews with a Dundee-Glasgow Queen Street relief train on 7 August 1965. *John Goss*

Wheezing steam from numerous leaking joints a former North British Railway 0-6-0 No 65282, built to a design dating from 1888, gently propels empty wagons from Bathgate to Riddoch Colliery in August 1965. Although these engines were used mainly for freight many carried names to commemorate battles and events of the first world war. *John Goss*

Isambard Kingdom Brunel was passionately convinced of the advantages of his 7ft 0¼in broad gauge which eventually extended from London to Penzance, South Wales and the Midlands. It was soon clear that operating inconvenience outweighed its advantages and the broad gauge had gone by 1892. While it lasted it gave the Great Western Railway that extra something which always made the GWR different from any other railway in the country then and since. In this photograph taken in the 1880s the signalman is displaying a white flag as a line clear indication to the driver of the approaching express which is headed by a 4-2-2 re-built from a former Bristol & Exeter railway 4-2-4 tank engine. The disc and crossbar signal at the platform end applies to the nearer track. *Collection of F. Moore Dutton*

As the broad gauge declined a third rail was added to provide mixed gauge which allowed the running of standard or broad gauge trains. The track work complications were absolutely frightful as can be seen in this photograph of a broad gauge express passing Flax Bourton near Bristol with a West of England-Paddington train in about 1890. In readiness for the final abolition of the broad gauge in 1892 many locomotives and coaches at this period were built in convertible form to allow the fitting of either broad gauge or standard gauge wheels.
Locomotive & General Railway Photographs

The removal of the broad gauge rail meant that many Great Western stations were left with ample clearance between tracks as here at Uphill near Weston-super-Mare with a standard gauge London-West of England train headed by one of William Dean's handsome 4-2-2s photographed around the turn of the century.
Locomotive & General Railway Photographs

The Great Western and its Western Region successor
were very fond of naming trains particularly during
the 1950s when named expresses on the Western
Region reverted to the old Great Western chocolate
and cream livery. Almost at the end of its journey
from Paddington is King class 4-6-0 No 6025 *King
Henry III* leaving St Annes Park Tunnel on the
outskirts of Bristol as it arrives with the Merchant
Venturer in the early 1960s.   *G. F. Heiron*

Fastest train on the Western Region in steam days
was the Bristolian between Paddington, Bath and
Bristol and while for a time in the 1950s the train
was in the hands of one of the then new BR standard
class 7 Pacifics, as for example No 70023 *Venus* seen
here leaving Bath, the train was more normally
worked by Castle class locomotives until dieselisation.
                                                G. F. Heiron

The last Great Western express passenger locomotive design was the County class introduced in 1945. Even these engines had the polished brass safety valve covers and copper caps to the chimneys that had adorned Great Western locomotives from time immemorial. Amid the Dartmoor foothills in South Devon No 1015 *County of Gloucester* assaults the final stage of the climb to Dainton summit between Newton Abbot and Totnes, one of the steepest main line gradients in the country. *T. E. Williams*

Edwardian elegance is portrayed in this photograph of a typical Great Western express during the first decade of the present century and seen in the open country near Acton. The locomotive is one of William Dean's Badminton class 4-4-0s No 3304 named *Oxford* gleaming from end to end and with polished brass dome and safety valve cover. The coaches are Dean's handsome clerestory roof type, standard from 1895 until about 1905.

Locomotive & General Railway Photographs

The Great Western Railway was always a believer in the publicity value of locomotive naming even for its many mixed traffic designs where the barrel was often scraped to find names of suitable houses or stately homes for its Hall, Grange and Manor classes. Several of the mixed traffic types have been preserved including Manor class 4-6-0 No 7808 *Cookham Manor* seen heading west into the evening sun near Twyford with a special from Taplow to Birmingham on 17 September 1966.

John Goss

Reflections on the water as a 51XX class 2-6-2T No 4157 heads the 1.40pm Hereford to Gloucester past Backney Halt on 17 October 1964.

John Goss

Absolutely evocative of the traditional country local train were the Great Western auto trains, often no more than a small 0-4-2 tank engine and one coach but sometimes, as here, two coaches, pushed in one direction and pulled in the other. They carried children to school and shoppers to nearby large towns and they provided connections off the expresses from London. Now they are no more and instead a dull uninteresting bus sometimes acts as a substitute. No 1458 propels its train out of Chalford for Gloucester on 19 September 1964.

John Goss

Close up of Great Western 2-6-0 No 6381 as it bursts out of Dinedor Tunnel with the 4.05pm Hereford-Gloucester train in June 1961.　　　*John Goss*

Probably the best known and well loved section of railway anywhere in the British Isles must be that along the coast between Dawlish and Teignmouth. This was the holiday line and as the train swept down alongside the waters of the Exe estuary excitement mounted when the train turned at Dawlish Warren to run right along the beach and at the foot of the weather-beaten red sandstone cliffs. Even if we were bound for Newquay or St Ives it seemed as if we were nearly there. Castle class 4-6-0 No 5035 *Coity Castle* runs along the sea wall with a Paddington-Penzance train in the mid-1930s.

Locomotive & General Railway Photographs

Hardly had we taken in the coastal view when the train swung inland up the Teign estuary to Newton Abbot where a stop was made to attach a second engine on to the train. The coast disappeared and soon the train was climbing hard up to Dainton summit, then followed a restrained run down the curves almost to sea level again at Totnes and the River Dart, and up again to the very edge of Dartmoor near Brent. Here 2-6-2T No 5158 and Castle class 4-6-0 No 5024 *Carew Castle* climb towards Dainton with the westbound Cornishman from Wolverhampton to Penzance on 3 September 1958.   *T. E. Williams*

Kings of the Royal Road: most passenger trains over
the steeply graded South Devon main line between
Newton Abbot and Plymouth needed double heading
but it was normally rare for two of the WR's most
powerful locomotives, the King class to be seen
together. No 6017 *King Edward IV* and No 6025
King Henry III leave Newton Abbot with the 10.35am
Paddington-Penzance on 14 September 1957.
                                    T. E. Williams

The single track cross-country line from Shrewsbury
to Aberystwyth and Pwllheli is now the only link
between the west coast of central Wales and the rest
of Britain. It includes some hard climbing to
Talerddig summit and while today it is the preserve
of local diesel units, in the 1960s in the final years of
steam, it carried a through named train, the Cambrian
Coast Express to Paddington which proved a tough
proposition for the BR standard class 4 4-6-0s which
saw out the last of steam working in that area. The
shed staff along the line were noted for their efforts
in trying to revive standards of cleanliness of former
years with their charges, as can be seen on No 75055
the lead engine of the pair heading the up Cambrian
Coast Express approaching Talerddig on 13 August
1956.   *John Goss*

Class 4 4-6-0 No 75024 was not so lucky since it had to handle the 10.30am Pwllheli-Paddington single handed on a wet drizzly day with greasy rails on the difficult climb to Talerddig also on 13 August 1956.
John Goss

This pair of locomotives virtually bridged the gap between the pioneer days of steam locomotives and the present time, for in their original form they were part of a delivery of suburban tank engines for local services in and out of Waterloo originally built in 1874/5. That three managed to survive until recent times despite the fact that the rest of the batch were withdrawn well before 1900 is little short of remarkable, except for the fact that the Southern Railway and its predecessors kept a number of old engines in service for specific services or branches. These three Beattie 2-4-0Ts were used on the china clay trains on the Wenford Bridge branch in Cornwall until they were displaced in the 1960s by more modern locomotives. Two of the trio Nos 30585/7 are seen at Hampton Court working an enthusiast's special on 2 December 1962. Both engines have been preserved.

D. T. Cobbe

Some of the most highly decorated locomotives in everyday service were found on the South Eastern & Chatham Railway which covered the whole of Kent and part of Sussex. In the years before the first world war most of the company's passenger locomotives were ornately lined out on a basically dark green ground colour with polished brass edging to wheel splashers and the whole surmounted almost like a crown by a massive brass dome. Here one of Wainwright's class D 4-4-0s, some say the most handsome engines ever built, storms through the outer London suburbs near Chislehurst on the climb towards the North Downs around 1910. Corridor trains were unknown on the SECR until the last year of its existence and even continental boat passengers had to make do with non corridor trains although a few compartments were served by toilets. The raised observatory for guards, known as the birdcage, harks back to the early days of railways when guards sat outside in the open perched up in a seat near the carriage roof.

Locomotive Publishing Company

Another very long-lived class of locomotive on the
Southern Railway was the Terrier 0-6-0T originally
built in 1872 for London suburban services. At least
a dozen survived well into the 1960s for use on
various branch lines including the Havant-Hayling
Island branch depicted here. Most of the Terriers
then extant have been preserved.   *John Goss*

Station in the middle of nowhere, or so it seems: this is Combpyne Halt on the Axminster-Lyme Regis branch. Here the branch train headed by a former LMS 2-6-2T No 41291 heads for Axminster in March 1965. Like most of the East Devon branches this one is now but a memory. *John Goss*

One line on the Isle of Wight between Ryde and
Shanklin survives under British Railways ownership
with an electric service of second-hand underground
trains. Indeed practically everything that ran on the
Isle of Wight railway system was second-hand, and
sometimes third-hand. The locomotive, No 26
Whitwell, blasting its way out of Newport for
Cowes on 13 November 1965 only a few weeks
before the end of the service, was another veteran
of a design originally produced in 1889 for London
& South Western suburban services.

John Goss

Another scene on the Ryde-Newport-Cowes line in
August 1965 as the fireman of class O2 0-4-4T No
24 *Calbourne* exchanges tokens for the single line
sections with the signalman at Havenstreet. The
hand exchange of tokens from a moving train was
a skilled operation which the rules laid down
should not be carried out at more than 10mph.
Although the Cowes line no longer exists the
section from Havenstreet to Wootton has been
preserved as a tourist attraction and so too has
No 24.

John Goss

Rebuilt West Country 4-6-2 No 34040 *Crewkerne* takes the curve near Pirbright Junction between Woking and Farnborough with a Waterloo-Bournemouth express on 10 September 1965.
John Goss

Express steam at Waterloo with another year to go: Oliver Bulleid was probably the most controversial locomotive designer of any on a British railway and introduced more novelties into his original Merchant Navy and West Country 4-6-2s in an endeavour to make a break from tradition. While many of the details failed miserably to come up to expectations nevertheless he produced engines that could make steam when wanted and could run fast. On the left No 34064 one of Bulleid's original Pacifics named with Battle of Britain associations in mind, this one was *Fighter Command*, waits to work the 9.33am relief train to Weymouth, alongside rebuilt Pacific No 34032 *Camelford* on the 9.30am train to Weymouth on 24 April 1965.   *John Goss*

Bulleid's heavier Pacifics, the Merchant Navy class, which originally appeared in wartime Britain during 1941 were also rebuilt during the 1950s to simplify maintenance and became one of the outstanding designs in Britain. No 35023 *Holland-Afrika* line leaves a cotton wool exhaust over the train as it heads south near Mortimer with the Pines Express from Manchester to Bournemouth on 13 November 1965. Sister engine No 35028 *Clan Line* has been preserved and is one of the few engines permitted to haul special excursions on British Railways.

Gerald T. Robinson

One of the few Southern Region suburban lines to remain unelectrified is the section from South Croydon to Oxted, Uckfield and Tunbridge Wells. Towards the end of the steam era on the SR it was one of the last steam worked sections with engines not always in the best of condition. In common with the few other surviving steam-worked London suburban lines in the early 1960s the voices of long suffering commuters were raised loud and clear at delays and failures, envying the seemingly more efficient electric services used by their colleagues living elsewhere. Class 4 2-6-4T No 80019 appears to be in good trim as it runs over Oxted Viaduct with a Tunbridge Wells West-Victoria train on 12 November 1955.   *Stanley Creer*

Boat train extraordinary: the Brockenhurst-Lymington branch takes to the water as it runs between Lymington Town and Pier stations where connections are made for the ferry to Yarmouth in the Isle of Wight. Here Ivatt 2-6-2T No 41203, an LMS designed type which subsequently spread to other areas of British Railways, was in charge of the branch train on 21 January 1967. This branch had the distinction of being the last to be worked by steam on BR and electric services took over in the summer of the same year.   *John Goss*

Few will not have some memories of railways, of
meetings, of partings, of happy events and sad
events, and in a century and a half the steam locomotive played its unobtrusive part in the lives of
many millions of people. The last journeys of well-
loved sovereigns from Queen Victoria to King George
VI were made by rail and Sir Winston Churchill
went to his final resting place in a funeral train from
Waterloo to Handborough. It was hauled by the
Battle of Britain locomotive named after him and is
seen here crossing the Thames at Richmond on 30
January 1965.   *G. M. Kichenside*

Seaside excursions were usually happy affairs but not when it was time to go home. Schools class 4-4-0 No 30924 *Haileybury* with a Ramsgate-Victoria return excursion climbs out of the Medway Valley up Sole Street bank and through the steeply sided chalk cutting of the North Downs on 18 June 1955.

Stanley Creer

In the days of steam most freight traffic was worked
basically in single wagon loads instead of the block
trains of today, and needed a network of marshalling
yards around London to shunt trains wagon by
wagon so that they reached their correct destinations.
From Feltham Yard, which served much of Southern
and South West England, transfer trips ran to
marshalling yards at Willesden and Stratford for
re-marshalling into trains for the North and North
East. Class H16 4-6-2T No 30520 seen leaving
Feltham in May 1954 spent most of its life on this
work or on working empty coaches between
Clapham Junction and Waterloo.

C. R. L. Coles

The Somerset & Dorset cross-country line between
Bath and Bournemouth was a remarkably useful but
an uneconomic link and like so many similar lines is
now but a memory. New Years Day 1966 saw class
5 4-6-0 No 73001 emerge from a cloud of steam at
Cole with a local train for Templecombe. Closure of
the line was scheduled for a day or so later, but in
fact it survived for another two months.

John Goss

In the Republic of Ireland steam locomotives disappeared on regular services a few years before they ceased on British Railways but on Northern Ireland Railways steam managed to hang on until the early 1970s. Even today, though, steam locomotives are occasionally used on excursions organised by railway societies and the less-heavily used Irish tracks give more opportunities for such things as photographic stops and run pasts. In this out of the carriage window shot of a Railway Preservation Society of Ireland special from Belfast to Dublin on 29 October 1966, a westerly wind carries the exhaust away from the train as it approaches Craigmore Viaduct on the climb towards Adavoyle between Portadown and Dundalk. *John Goss*

Contrasting carriage window shot from a Machynlleth-Shrewsbury train climbing Talerddig Bank on 9 July 1966 behind class 4 4-6-0 No 75004. *John Goss*

Main line steam power can still be sampled in action
on British Railways main lines on occasional special
excursions. One of the locomotives kept in tip-top
condition for this sort of work is the first of the
GWR King class locomotives built in 1927, No 6000
King George V, which retains the bell with which it
was presented on its visit to America in 1927. It is
seen here approaching Twyford with a special
excursion on 7 October 1971.   *John Goss*

Two Castle class locomotives have been preserved in working order; one, No 4079 *Pendennis Castle*, dates from the original batch of GWR Castle class engines built in 1923, the other seen here, No 7029 *Clun Castle*, is the last of the class to be built in a final batch constructed after the second world war. Here it is working an enthusiast special on the return journey from Birkenhead to Birmingham in March 1967. It is normally kept at Tyseley Depot, near Birmingham.   *John Goss*

Another of the former LNER class A4 streamliners which can be still seen in action is No 60019 *Bittern* seen here on a rail tour around Lancashire on a very murky 25 November 1967.   *Mike Turner*

One of the earliest standard gauge branches to be resuscitated by a preservation society for passenger working was the Bluebell Line between Sheffield Park and Horsted Keynes in Sussex. Although most of the locomotives and the rolling stock come from the Southern Railway and its constituents there are quite a number of items representing other railways including this GWR 4-4-0 No 3217 *Earl of Berkeley* seen in action during 1969.   *John Goss*

One of the most active of the preserved Irish loco-
motives is a former Great Southern & Western 0-6-0
No 186 which is frequently used on Railway
Preservation of Ireland excursions. It is seen here at
Crumlin on 28 October 1967.   *John Goss*

Unique in Britain is the Snowdon Mountain Railway,
still entirely steam worked and with Swiss built
locomotives, some dating back from the opening of
the railway in 1896. Speeds are low and where more
than one train is needed for a particular timetabled
service because of heavy traffic, several trains may be
run following one another at a minimum distance
apart. The locomotive is always at the lower end and
pushes the coach uphill.   *John Goss*

The Isle of Man Railway, which once had an
extensive 3ft gauge network covering many parts of
the island has been cut back over the years until now
it operates over only a short section of the Port Erin
line as a tourist attraction. It reached its centenary
in 1973 and some of the locomotives and coaches
date right back to this period although as services
have been curtailed so fewer engines and coaches
have been required in traffic. 2-4-0T No 11 *Maitland*
climbs towards Port Soderick with the 10.35am
Douglas-Port Erin on 2 July 1973.   *John Goss*

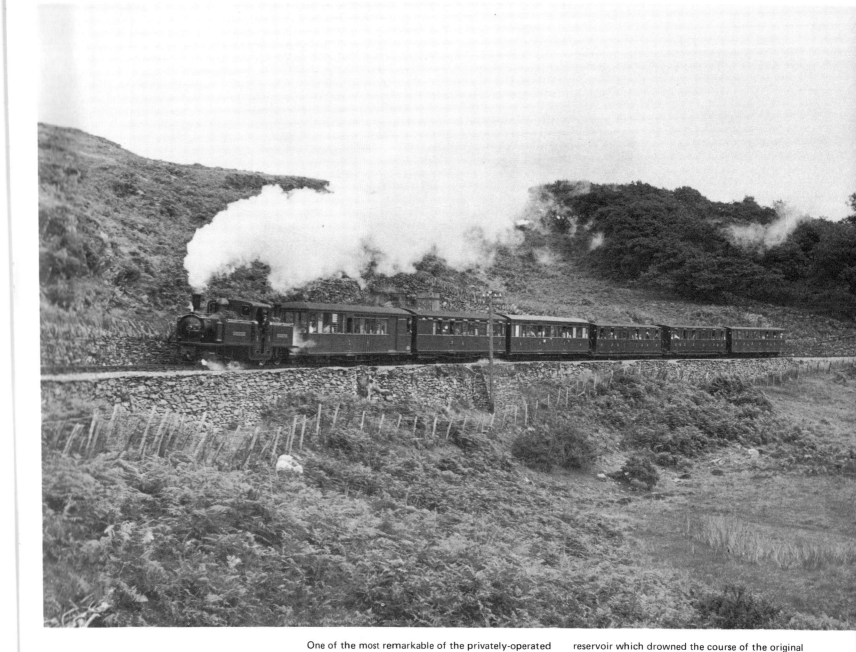

One of the most remarkable of the privately-operated steam railways today is the Festiniog, the 1ft 11½in gauge line which runs from Porthmadog to Dduallt high up over the Vale of Festiniog. Apart from its unique locomotives, which include the only examples of the Fairlie articulated type to run in Britain today, the trains despite their narrow width include corridor coaches, buffets and observation cars. Today a new line is being built above Dduallt to skirt a new reservoir which drowned the course of the original line to Blaenau Ffestiniog the original terminus of the line and which the railway aims to reach within a few years. This and most of the privately-operated steam railways running today are supported by active groups of volunteers who have a hard task in maintaining the lines and their stock in tip-top condition as popular tourist attractions.

John Goss

Memories of steam at Waterloo in the 1960s. While
steam in everyday service on British Railways might
be a memory, as the preceding pages have shown
steam still lives. It has survived for a century and a
half and in private hands looks good for many more
years yet.   *Kenneth Field*

One of the most remarkable of the privately-operated steam railways today is the Festiniog, the 1ft 11½in gauge line which runs from Porthmadog to Dduallt high up over the Vale of Festiniog. Apart from its unique locomotives, which include the only examples of the Fairlie articulated type to run in Britain today, the trains despite their narrow width include corridor coaches, buffets and observation cars. Today a new line is being built above Dduallt to skirt a new reservoir which drowned the course of the original line to Blaenau Ffestiniog the original terminus of the line and which the railway aims to reach within a few years. This and most of the privately-operated steam railways running today are supported by active groups of volunteers who have a hard task in maintaining the lines and their stock in tip-top condition as popular tourist attractions.

John Goss

Memories of steam at Waterloo in the 1960s. While
steam in everyday service on British Railways might
be a memory, as the preceding pages have shown
steam still lives. It has survived for a century and a
half and in private hands looks good for many more
years yet.   *Kenneth Field*